Hawk

and

Vivian Ayers

ISBN: 978-1-63804-091-0

First published in 1957.

This edition published by
Clemson University Press
116 Sigma Dr.
Clemson, SC 29634

Designed and typeset by Lindsay Scott.
Cover design based on a design by Betty Jo Jones
Cover image and all interior images by John Biggers.

*To those who would rise above
the slumber of the night—*

*To those who would dare!
Take wings*

CLEMSON
UNIVERSITY
PRESS

To—

JOHN BIGGERS

Whose inspired drawings are
a rival account. Yes, Johnny
those were very happy days.

Introduction

Astronaut Michael Collins, upon his return to Earth after the 1969 Apollo 11 mission, said that a future flight would best include "a priest, a philosopher, and a poet." Then, he said, "we might get a much better idea of what we saw."

Only a poet can describe the magnificence of space.

As young children, we understood that Vivian Ayers, our mother, was a poet—a published poet (*Spice of Dawns*, 1953). In the pre-dawn hours of morning, while we were sleeping and the world was quiet, she did her "work," and it was serious business. We knew to respect that, even without understanding the full measure of the work and its meaning. It was serious business.

Vivian Ayers was on a mission: a quest for freedom, and not for herself alone. Much of this work was shared with us as it was unfolding. She would throw forth a phrase:

"Be true! Be beautiful! Be free!" "Force nothing! ...... let things transpire!"

and we would repeat it with vigor. Her verse was fluid, dancing to its own rhythm and cadence. She even invented words or created new interpretations of them by virtue of their spelling in her text. "The poet is not bound by convention!" she would say. Her language, pure and precise, evoked grandeur.

Hawk, three years in its making, was published in 1957: eleven weeks before the launch of Sputnik.

One may ask, "How did a young woman from the mill town of Chester, South Carolina, living in Houston, Texas with three young children in the mid-twentieth century, come to compose this long-form poem, an allegory of freedom that references space flight even before lift-off of the world's first space craft? How did she depict scenes so vividly that some twenty-odd years later excerpts of her text would be photographed, enlarged, and exhibited in Space Hall at the Lyndon B. Johnson Space Center?"

What cause sparked this effect?

One might answer that maybe the "spark" was Vivian Ayers's exposure to classical literature while a student at Brainerd Institute, Barber-Scotia College, or Bennett College; or maybe it was her interest in Eastern philosophy, cultural traditions of peoples indigenous to the Americas, or ancient lore from the African continent; or perhaps it was something more fundamental—simply the longing of the soul to experience truth of its "Self-," that inner landscape which calls forth the manifestation of the material world.

The poet, you see, is guided by inspiration, intuitive thought. Thought is not an empty proposition, an idling of the mind and senses. Oh, no! Thought is dynamic, creative force that leads to lofty—or lowly—places.

To honor poet Vivian Ayers's 100th Birthday, we are pleased to present this second publishing of *Hawk* through Clemson University Press. We are thankful to Dr. Alison Mero for her unwavering commitment to this publishing. Also, we acknowledge and offer salutations to Pete Stone, a dear friend, a young "Hawk," whose support has been critical to the success of this printing.

On behalf of Debbie Allen Nixon, Hugh Welburn Allen, and Andrew "Tex" Allen, Jr.,

Phylicia Rashad

Apology

Every Hawk has his haunts...and mine is Freedom. I am the very sense of 'pursuit of freedom'. Time and space, and sphere upon sphere have surrendered to my selective gaze—and lucky stroke of rapacious skill.

And yet in offering this scroll, it seems that never before in any quest have I been so encumbered with other Hawks, who— not because they were selected but out of their own free wills—have espoused the pursuit; and may thus make just claims on its rewards. I think of:

Edward R. Uhlan, president of Exposition Press ... Elizabeth Allen Griffin, poet and friend... Dr. Daniel T. Skinner, linguist giving the go-signal for new words... Dr. H. I. Fontellio-Nanton, journalist always near comes time to edit another script... Maxine Savant Farnum, introducing new studies...Dr. Mary Jourdan Atkinson, giving the incalculable boost of Anthropology...the Perellas, Lee and Paul, submitting criticisms, and lee, kind and intuitive, typing drafts as my own zest waned toward the finish... Mr. and Mrs. R.D. Ayers keeping an avid interest...three little winglings Deborah, Phylicia and Andrew A. Allen, who for many months slept to the tatter of a typewriter...a reflective giver of flowers who so showered every plateau... a man called Flannagan... and really an incredible number of others.

And so I must apologize for having found no escape complete ... but I am still quite fluid, and this world is asleep with transpirations yet undreamed of—

Hawk

SEQUENCE

Discarnit Guard

Mutation

Migration

Swan Song of Migration

Transmigration

Earth Electric

Operation: Inspiration Minus

ROSTER

Hawk...assuming reincarnation-that soul stuff is indestructible, carrying on from one beingness to another...is narrated from the planet **Saturn** by Hawk.

Hawk...a discarnit one, operating from the level of Cestral mind, is appointed Guard of Sleep; and while enroute to Mars on an Hierarchical mission, stops over to Saturn...for a little breather, a little snow, and maybe a breath of wine.

Gator—of the species Alli...an old friend to Hawk since the days Hawk lived on Saturn; and affectionately called Red Eyes, has been on the lookout for Hawk; and straggles up shortly after Hawk settles to Saturn. Gator likes having Hawk tell him stories; for after all, he never gets off the planet and — according to Hawk — Hawk goes everywhere.

On the occasion of this meeting the two make a proposition: Gator is to be more — generous with his· wine: and Hawk will tell a story. Hawk then proceeds to tell of having once. been a **Man** on **Earth** ... and with the bent on **Freedom**.

Fervour...is freedom plus effort, plus the surge of something wonderful within ...

And **jim**...is a devine arm, reached out to guide one of the crude effort - but finest aspiration - to attainment of perfection and bliss.

Hawk

Discarnit Guard

...? O...there is someone?

Red Eyes! Of all beings— Hi! I heard shuffling there in the snow....Where are you going?

...to see me? You knew all along I would come?

Well, I am surely here in the dense self, if that is what you mean... I have stood in love for some snow. But in awakening, I am as ever firm in cultless wisdom and awareness.

How are things on Saturn? I see the Turtles are still singing the blues, complaining of their old shells.... And the flock?...Have they fared all through the solstice?

Yes, I heard your ring system fell, and you've had terrific snows. But I would have come anyway. I rarely resist Saturn, if I'm passing. You should see it from space...spinning like a disk of sapphire—

But tell me, how did you know I was coming?

I figured as much... You were looking for me. Ears for adventure...and Hawk would have some stories—

Well, yes, I have been rather constantly on the go. In and out of Orion...to Leo —to Virgo —to Capricorn... stalked around some on the Earth's weedy Moon; but quietly, avoiding all monsters—you know.

...you inquire into everything Gator. But I guess I should tell you this: I am the newly appointed Guard of

Sleep. I stand Guard over all sentiments of rest; and I have what I call govern Moons, Moons which persuade the temperaments of a given sphere...and so carry out much of the plan while I work out the essential wherefores of each cycle.

Earth's Moon was fairly still, except for a conference of Souls...there was much talk of its being invaded from Earth. And a prize offered the best suggestions for what to do with it as Earth territory. I suggested they reserve it a resort for those diplomats on Earth adding stealth and avarice. The smell of Moon grass breeds lust for money...and they could loll around under the trees and sate with greed.

...parable? What parable?

...gold to the ground, again to become as useless to men as of yore it had been.

No, I don't remember any such parable. A cup of wine might strengthen my recall; but— well, it matters...it matters.

Now look at you scuffling.....Sure as Inkling I knew you had a flask hid somewhere there in the woods. Still the old dipso-humn? Still the ol' dipso.

What's that?...I am still Truth's Hawkward beam?

Hah, Gator; I sure wish you'd get busy and do something.

...like what? Like anything. No one's stopping you but you.

All right, you don't have to explain yourself. I know you can't **just leave**...it takes grit to free yourself.

By all means...finish picking the illusions of Saturn before you leave...

But if I were you, I wouldn't take forever. **Someone** intends to subdue this culture, and in no uncertain terms....One day there'll be aircraft hovering over, spitting fire from the belly...and so low you can see observers taking notes. They will fly as easily backward as forward...

O— there will be a raid, all right. There's going to be one...and it won't be any great tragedy, in spite of all the commotion and scrambling, and running. I mean it can't be any terrific loss to the Universe. It will take whatever mind stuff here is in fairly good condition, and use it someplace else.

No, I won't be any place around, Gator. One must be unencumbered and on the move. I can't identify with any one family. I must maintain identity with the whole...

And I'm on the way to Mars. I must be in the sphere before it eclipses Jupiter. A leader of the young reckless there is mounting vanity beyond vanity; and the moon can't handle him; and-well, I'll know what to do with him. He needs a certain therapy to sober his ego.

Is he a serious frolic?

He fairly is a frolic of itself....How can I **'just tell him'**? The seeds of my own food are not enough for people— But I can handle him. What I'll do is get him in love with some damsel; and then snatch it away from him! That will sober him up full quick.

O yes!...He will cry to heaven that someone's done him an injustice...

But the great one's patience is a little longer than mine, **It** will pamper him. **It** hath much patience with the carnit mind.

If the living would only remember...**justice** is not so much a matter of regal mind as it is of immutable Kosmic laws— which just operate! I mean they don't care who breaks them, they just operate...

Now Gator, what is it you're about? If you hide that flask, I will tell you nothing more...not a shred. Nothing!...and I was just about to explain the order of things...

There is a rumour you know that Heaven stacked the stars according to the sun's riles fancy ...but it's so far from the truth. Those of us – undeluded – know...

...apologies!...it did seem you were making off with it....Set it here between us, then there'll be no question...

Those of us – undeluded – know the cause was really... a rhapsody! Every star yet hums reverberations of the theme—

...was I **there?**

Where you there, Gator, when Lizards fell to sports like hunting and fishing which are basically immature? Were you **there**?

But you can recapitulate the process, can't you?

Well, this is what you're smart for...god!...What do

you think you're smart for?

Come on, fill the cup... To youth— to wine—
to love— and to truth ! ...agh!
... the very statement of ecstasy!

Yes it comes to me now, —**bloated and dead on
the beach they lay...**

You going to drink some?... Swell.

**...uncared for, unguarded, unclaimed by a soul...
cast into the sea— the scaly worm...**

Yes. —but please!...nothing quite so astral. I am in a
mood for cestral truth.

Here is one, Red Eyes, from the region of great you-
likes. A favourite with souls, it is a compendium of the
consciousness in the back of every being— but you must
pretend you don't have an old mind!

Come closer....Are you willing to pretend you don't
have an old mind?

Let's make believe you were younger— years
younger...and went to a show, adding to it reciprocally;
and going to come in all aired and proper...

Now:

Every star yet hums reverberations of the theme!
And the show opens...with arms of ecstasy...

Swell....Pause!

Settle.

— MUTATION

It was April...

What difference does it make what time, Gator?

...all right, 2052. That was as great a year as any for the great.

But look, Gator, this show is beyond superficial insistences such as a calendar. If there's any time involved, it's a matter of transpirations, you know...the real substantial happenings of the kosmos.

...Calendar?

Oh, that's a relic from Man's vernacular. I haven't used it since I left Earth.

Yes...but I have lived on Earth. I was Man once... twice to be exact. And this show opens on Earth.

No, it was my decision to go. I wanted to go. Earth looks good from a level of non-involvement ... if you're just looking in, it'll get you. It has a hard and crusty surface; in fact it sort of resembles you...and there's family life, all kinds of professions, love, art, and science —if you just look in it'll get you.

...it was my decision to leave. We'll get to all of that; but wait. First you must hear of the prevailing superstitions ...a little wine, please... They, as much as anything, I would say, precipitated my successes.

Earth was a demention of **Hell**, if you know what I mean; that's another one of percussions.

The unsane so far outnumbered the sane that even **Tolerance** got over on their side. Even **Tolerance**. Sane ones, not being able to take it, quibbled off their quids, were locked up, labeled **insane** and given treatment...the unsane working on the insane —umph!

The most amusing were the 'authorities.' Little folks compelling little folks to revere their squalid opinions, find reward in their paltry emanations, and even fear them. At times it seemed they were at least mimicking a second-hand impression of Nature's behavior in the Universe; but still it was very amusing.

Success was there, but most folk had it by the tail. They thought from outer beingness in rather than from inner beingness out. They thought success were some outer thing throwing out light to the person...and not some inner thing throwing out light. So naturally, as you would expect, they were forever scrapping like their dogs - over forms and stuff they could never possess anyway.

But they were **smart**. Generically, they would invent some panacea, like a sprawling and elaborate tax system ... designed to give all parties concerned greater communal benefits, and leisure, and pleasure... And then proceed, from the moment of invention, to get caught up in the damned thing...thereafter spending the greater portion of their leisure being victim to the purely tabulative side of it, or being chastised and penalized for not being victim.

In some places they put the weirdest twist on sex. So that if you were a female exhibiting real talent for anything else, they labeled you a bitch and what they meant was "undersexed." I often wondered if they thought Christ had come to save men or women.

This is no mere astral yarn. It happens yet; and if you're wondering how they kept it all up, I'll tell you. They had the situation controlled...so that when you came, you couldn't say a word for the first six months ... and by the time they taught you the words that said what they wanted to hear, you had also learned not to contradict them.

Truth, they harnessed and barned in the stockyard **Idealistic**...for the majority of Men feared standing alone...as if they could! or could not.

All things on Earth seemed in order except Man. Between reason to wisdom, and the ability to err...Man's free will permits him to disorder.

I got so I avoided them almost completely, a lot of mixed, egotistical — well they had more mis-misappropriated pride and reason than anything else, I felt.

They exalted the infectious ego; put laurels about its sick ear...and used their best found modes of communication to keep each other puffed, and maintain the confusion.

You wouldn't handle a silver flask with hammers and nails — would you? You wouldn't take a crystal cup and dash it against a rock...then saunter around claiming it wasn't strong or valuable because it was vulnerable? You wouldn't do that would you? But they did...and especially in the area of creative efforts...where progress literally comes from. Yes...of course there was some inadvertence, but others knew just what they were doing ... the sorry bastards. I thought they had a lot of nerve to set themselves up even as Satan. Even Satan has a certain hypothetical function. Even he will inspire one to avoid pollution.....I got sick of the hammer and nail treatment.

Then, having accomplished all havoc they would equate things by saying everything happens for the best ... **"Everything happens for the best"**...and that was the lie. Ordinarily things happen in my life the way I make them happen; and things happen in life according to the way you make them happen. The great difference between you and me is in the way we make things happen. And it can't possibly be for the best unless our intentions are for the best.

They pretended so carnit much...building up a kind of collective false security. And came time to make a real decision; they acted as if they were scared to live and afraid to die.

Well to get on, and frankly, after twenty some odd years of that one variety of hell...I was just plain weary... of struggling, and struggling, and struggling— and for what? I thought. It's hardly worth it.

It could easily have been a hopeless situation... because I was tired and painful...dazed with pain. My depress was stacked; and I felt like a puddle of grey soup, practically ready to commit my record to the rocks...it was driving me west! I had to get lost or found, or damned near clear of the mess.

And then it happened...the very lucid transpiration.

I found myself unaccountably possessed by a strange, enchanting kind of restlessness ... that seemed to elevate the mind, and purify the heart- and make the whole world hang together!

There was a new excitement in every old thing.
And asleep or awake, there stirred incessantly within a
caustic state of desiring, and scintillating fervour. My
heart had a new beat- and a new tune,

Everything I see and do
Turns to thoughts of you...
           —strange monot'ny.
Just what was I to do
With this Moon— and no you?
           = strange monot'ny.

It was monotous, it was precarious, it was strange...
and like one dying of thirst, I could not drink deeply
enough. I, incontinent, did wish more fervour still...and
all the world—and everything! was us.

I felt strong enough to change the whole world! ... I
felt strong enough to change!

...and my fancy went wild!

First I thought to become a frog. Then I could be as
sane as I liked, and no one would suspect it or consider
it a threat...and I could live on any continent in the
world...and prance prance around in the nude...in the
water and out of the water—

...but that would be impostrous!

I would be too small to protect myself, and all the
cocky primates would misuse me as prey.

Then I decided to be something inanimate like...fire.
Yes, fire! I could lurk in little unnoticed places and when
people weren't looking, I could leap out and ravish all the
dry musty things they valued most ... HAGH!

... a stuffy old society matron outdoors helplessly wailing, while I made a meal of her antique sofa!

Yes, I would be fire!...the subtlest sovereign of an empire. I would lend them my assistance if I liked the way things went; or if I didn't, I could withdraw taking my share of things with me... leaving man to bare-handed impoverishment!

But this too was impostrous!

If I ever got caught in the rain— one of those impatient hurricanes...it would be the death of me!

And then one night— unwittingly— I walked out, looked up, and discovered a diamond studded sky.

Look at that! I thought, **A world resplendent with beauty and truth...and dignity, and freedom!**

It was the first time I had ever really seen it... and the perfect scheme then crystalized in my mind: I would convert this energy to the wings and take to the stratosphere. I'd soar up there!

I could find no information on the modification of Sapiens. I was left pretty much to my own wits; I must admit, however, being a natural for the challenge.

Presently I had the solution— a bird life apprenticeship! And spotted the tree. It was a giant of an Elm with broad limbs and lots of foliage.

I climbed up and perched on a limb to stay, rejecting all Sapien modes of locomotions; except for a twice daily routine of running very swiftly and taking off into extended leaps.

Mutation

I lent all my centers to solemn concentration, banking heavily on the power of concentration; but to give it full persuasion, I also fasted. Just early in the downs before sunrise, I would get down and scratch around for worms.

To begin with, it was a lonely existence, for I made no sense to people, and less to the birds. But I scoffed at both of them. Before long, the birds would not only seek my society, but mimic my behavior as that of a grander species. And the people...'mm, the people. There were very few gods on Earth, and mostly people. They stood around and gaped as if they thought I were queer...and I pitied them equally for being quite so impotently fixed to their tired answers, ancient dogmas, and assumed manners...After awhile some came closer, requesting information, and pretending to really be interested, you know. But I wouldn't talk to them. I knew these bastards would come and detain; and then be first to complain and criticize if I couldn't make it.

Besides my heart was busy...and lift with Fervour —

I could do anything. I could change the whole world for you...and I would! Just tell me how you want it. Would you rather blue trees? and a green sky?

This is so wonderful—so wonderful! So much more wonderful than I could ever say..... But I don't want to say it. I wouldn't like to have to. Just let me be what I want to be .... Do you remember what it was not to have this? Do you remember that we couldn't do the things we wanted to before?...that you couldn't be what you wanted to be? Oh, let's make the most of it. Let's be strong! Let's be free!

All things bursting with inspiration, nothing seemed Insurmountable. Even loud-mouthed thunderstorms and their rioting rains were nulled.

There would come great claps of thunder!...and light playing everywhere. The air would cool; and tree tops rustle with high winds. The birds would pipe and perch closer together; and people would run for cover...but I never moved; I just sat there.

Never! Would I return to the unsimplicated lot of Sapiens. I would be the greatest free-est wingling in all the milky way! My trails would rack the stars.

For forty-eight days and nights I fasted, seldom getting hungry after the first several days. I just ate to keep the body warm and working on its transmutation.

And then came the memorable forty-ninth dawn ... The first sharp call of day pierced the dawn, and I was rousing as usual to scratch for worms.

Standing up to stretch and bending my head back toward the sky, I was aware of something — of a clinch on the tree, on the branch beneath me.... For moments it was rather like some facet of concentration, I had concentrated for so long. But on waking furthur and glancing down, I could see that my feet had webbed... my toes were webbed...and prim and clinching! It was lavender...amazing!...a real substantial change! My dream was coming true. My prayers were getting through...and I found myself erecting spontaneously— in praise. And I raised my arms to make an expression of thanks...but there were no arms! High on the thorax there were little white wings! It was a wonder...it was a miracle!

And I hopped from branch to branch, trying out the wings and whistling happy tunes, and just being very amazed and greatful... I could fly. I was free! Earth would be lost moss off a cannon ball—

And from that moment on, I looked away from it all ... and I thought, **"Thank god ... thank god...there is a sky..."**

Wherever an instrument salute!
Portends itself in quest of Truth,
   Truth-ebullient!
throws out a bouyant mat
that it should tread...

I looked to the sky...and let the want of it flow through my being, as I generated more and more want of it ... sending the best formed images of my hopes flowing into it ... sustaining the flow of desiring, and holding my mind steady in the stream of vibrations.

And the swelling sea of fervour...let go tides of want and power...

The heart breathed ready... limbs throbbed with vigour....One stout boost from my slender shanks ... and going, going, gone! into the soothing winds, I was off!

...but not long boastful.

Earth's atmosphere — to say the least was the least auspicious to a neophyte. For her regular airborne realities sensed up, obscuring the event of my coming.

My young wings flickered like an old fashioned reel. I swirled excessively and constantly feared a plummeting back to Earth. I would sweep my wings forward as far as I could — and beat hard down to the hips...but many a wind I winged at wasn't there anymore and I was the silhouette of a dipping kite. I hated myself for being so ignorant of intemperate pressures, and capricious winds, and the myriad attitudes a wing must therefore be prepared to take.

Those winds weren't aware of me at all. Except for the drafts of warming currents, I wouldn't have had a chance. And having once considered wings the battle won, I gleaned from these happenings this was only the beginning....I let up a supplication for greater self control,

Grant me the wit from hub to tip
to know when a swirl is spent
For even prayer, if overdone
may find its power bent.

...oh, before I got it said, an engaging warmth brushed in close; and commenced radiating meanings.

No, no words, just meanings. But pertaining to flight, as if some eye had been watching all the time.

For as long as it was there, it kept saying in its way, that anxiety and fear were negative attitudes brought up from earth...but survival in the air rather called for the response of positive stroking.

...at the time? I didn't exactly know, Gator. I didn't know if it were the one great anima of existence or a scout.... But I used the information and learned to stay aloft as easily as any other creature in the air. So I counted him a friend...and thereafter I called him **jim**.

Of course I now suspect it was some agent throwing me a mat — a life-line from Truth via Radiation ... that secret of circles dictating forms with frequencies, so that in one caprice it was worms, in yet another — wind, or a Man, or a tree....Well, let's not pull any punches; I am damned sure Kosmic Radiation knows what it's doing...But let us not lend transparency where aestheticism demands the naked eye.

All through the sky there are winds that come to usher one onward; but then come winds to jeopardize. and blow you back again ...

No Hawk wings steadily forward. You can make the most of every energy that flows —achieving rise to relative sentations of exhiliration and ecstasy....But as pinions furl and ambition nods, ecstasy wanes, and only the pangs of inecstasy can spawn the flight to ecstasy again.

Filled to the self's capacity, Hawks sing in breath of ecstasy. After climbing fairly high, and finally producing an unbroken spiral, I lifted to a plateau and gave the first spontaneous song. To any listening ears, it may have sounded somewhat harsh, but to me it was music... my impiracle analysis of a wonderful world asleep with transpirations yet undreamed of:

...in the beginning, there was conflict!

I was impatient with waning ecstacy. It seemed a waste — a nullifying waste. At the outset, moments of back-some induced a sentiment of rest. And damned near maddening it was, to contend with slumber and checked drive when I would rather have kept going. But that was the order of things. Every finished spiral makes its round of all sentiments of being.

But always — once again, spawned the flight to ecstasy again; and it always was significantly another transpiration.

...you can't tell the difference between positive and negative?

Sure you can.... Positive means you recognized the power there is; and negative means you don't recognize **It**. To the extent you recognize **It**, **It** recognizes you, and–

...if you don't?...

...no pinions far. No wings. You just remain a flub. That's what...**It** also invented the ego, you know. You can scarcely protect yourself without paying sufficient homage...

Now what's so unhappy about that? Smile...and let's go another mile.

Happiness could be called the art of self protection. For the more one communicates with Truth, the more she permits you to know of self protection. First she permits one small view and then another...full recognition permitted only in the **May of coming**.

But the steed of flight was Fervour.

Morning, noon, and night, Fervour kept me in vigour and zest ... jesting through the work of lifting, inspiring songs in sentiments of ecstasy, aid rearing to go in the moments of backsome.

High above clouds visible to Earth, I cruised the fairer skies. With each plateau of spiral being more exhilarating than the last; even in wild moments of waning ecstasy, the Sun kept shining through. There seemed nothing but space and spiraling between me and the stars.

...yes, I kept going days and nights; all of it was equally exciting. At the close of day.   — the sun, dropping like a bouncing ball of razed ruby would take a last look at the world and bounce low. The adjutant Moon would then sit up proud! and there in heaping dusk and the twilight of vesper, would collect all of the Sun's old intimates.

Discounting effort, I winged with effusive drive. I could hardly have done otherwise. The sky kept making definite commitments which I could hear:

> **...for those of you who lift and create songs to benefit stilled lust: I will benefit your desires. and never say die —**

And I piped with growing passion for...just a little nook among the stars... with Fervour.

But you must know ... there is no pretense in the sky! If one stays aloft in the air, it is because he copes with air. It doesn't know about tongue service, laurel bearers, and advocates. You either make some real progress or you don't.... Shocking! was the comparison of this reality with those I had abandoned. The impact of assembled feelings inspired gruelling strains...

> **Christianity**
> **is still**
> **the dull**
> **and pretentious lady—**

Till now, I am not impressed with the aim of priests and Clergy, whose aim is — at best — a seething thing.

Yes. I kept going. The stride was constant effort.

To pick yourself up and over clouds, through the air is a feeling of real power, and self control...it's like stroking up in cotton that gets finer and finer; and the truest sensation of traveling. For the first time you would be aware of really going someplace.

I was sold...gone! And there was no doubt in my mind that at a certain altitudes Space would, on the score of my intent, let down her carpet of magnetism and lure me onto an intimate reception....**Me, the lofty one, winging eventless to Olympus ...**

But it was just another level of bland success, which some adorn...but for which Truth has little use and less regard...

And so on one chilly night, soared into an area more turbulent than the rest.

I wasn't long in the cool that night before suspecting the stars would not collect; for the sky was mighty brown and an ominous still crept in the place of splendour. and as I flew on, it grew so cold I thought sure to condense to an icedrop...

Worse still, there was an ebb in the feel and warmth of Fervour...and just a very arid sense of being and of going...? but surely **Fervour** would never leave me...

Every kind of uncertainty vexed...as the night collected elements of dubious intent.

Mood in match with mood...there were poised and threatening thunderheads...spook lights ... monstrous meanings...eyes without eyes...daunted hopes...utter aloneness...dismay... anxiety...and tears.

Could I have misgoverned myself with Fervour? Could I have offended her?.... there were phrases not well sung. I had neglected to dwell upon her importance to me. Heavens!. ... She was sensitive and highly impressionable. There were several slopes I had winged badly.!! When she returned I would handle every gale as though it were my sole creation. ...Vagrant! an ordinary vagrant she was. I would have nothing more to do with her!.... Perhaps her natural stride was Freedom; if so, she had a perfect right to it....But god! self protection! I could not afford to free her; she was the very hope of my existance—

I would not look for her; that would not be sane. Restraint!! I would make the contact when the contact came...

...or would the Kosmos have some hand in this ?...

Could it be I was to gain self mastery, with or without Fervour?....Perhaps bogging down in sentiments was an invitation to have them snatched away... Restraint !!

...or was I being impelled to some higher expression?

Way up, that high, winds crossed each other in great wispy streaks...and getting worse progressively, commenced howling at the prows like monsoons...and barbing the area with tons of speed!

They kept of entire stratum roped like Hegelian scribbling ...

I put a wing in, and they tossed me somer-saulting back - off keel - to lighter gales...It scared the snuggings out of me!

Holy Cow! I thought...**this must be the monster that culls dreamers from their dreams; and sends them plummeting back-forever to the never-do.**

And up popped that old demon, anxiety, again. It seemed I would fairly abandon myself, and then attempt to do what could only be done with the self.

I made all manner of mental notes, and symbols for do's and don'ts, mostly don'ts.

—Restraint — a medium of assistance—

—Make every flip of the wing count—

—Mistakes too costly—

—Build determination—

—Let no residual concepts, ghosts of living done long ago, tamper with the right of a flaming heart ...

And after much of this kind of sane self collecting, an echo — quite whimsical and impassive — came through from somewhere there in the maze—

... excell — or I shall never return to you ...

It was the voice of Fervour!...she was still there!!...a Caspian strain in the muck and maze... and the spell was on...

Feeling myself nothing without her. I knew I would scuffle to excell in her estimation. For any hope without her was vain— was barren. She was the gift out of

Migration

which I had given world acceptance; every gain in altitude had been an expression out of the suitability of our union...every display of verve and ability, a reference to it.

I would brave those raucous winds...I would brave hell and pandemonium if I must. This way at least I waited for her....If it should take a thousand nights to win— what were a thousand nights? ... Deported from the scene knowing she would never return, there would be nothing ... it would be less than Hell...Night upon night would amount to nil. This way at least I waited for her.

I was sure my fear would subside. Hope and pride would take care of that. But there is no course through anxiety to poise. And the bare unimaged thought...of having come so far... abandoned, hope, feared, believed, and glimpsed the lilt pleasures of success...all this! only to meet failure and regression, was enough to obliterate the senses. It was impostrous!

I had come a long way, and I couldn't go back....

Trouble had taught me to pray and I cried out loud,

God do something!...do something...

A quickening impulse rushed through me in that instant!

And there were shafts of radiation...jim...and aphorisms:

Increase your inner strength...Rise to level above bland desire...Did you ever hear of the plow?...
...bland desire? the plow? Surely there wasn't anything

I neglected to want? But jim's words were definitely to the need, always...and a fount of courage.

Yes, I saw him — but not with these eyes. I knew him as intimately as you would know a pain across the brow. It was he who told me about values. I had a reverence for him I felt never could express except by being as great a wingling as I had vowed to be.

jim's words were fluid strength. I collected strength as I pondered his counsel. There **was** some **higher expression** to be achieved...and the implication was that I could win. My resources fell into one pact for survival... And I hawked the assault! the seige was on...

I soared head-on into the thick of it — defying every threat of it and ghostly terror.

The great winds raced and hummed like god-bees ... and my heart hammered like an anvil. I sparred with the forbearance of a winner, which I dared any obstacle to match.

I raced on in spite of every droning rift and took rest in their god-blamed breezes...

But just when things built, as it were, to the seeming last hilt of progress and — wholly charged — I thought to go plummeting through...

...the winds drew their lethal muscles: and lashed the sky with a scathing power, superceding all former terror...

Roughed up, they tossed me around for more than a league...and commenced blowing off some of my hard fledged feathers!

I managed to straighten...and then I swore! —by my right to dream! to surprise this killer with a little taste of rebate...and beat him at his game, and wake him up! to the rights of dreamers.

The winds were so rough and raucous I couldn't face them but never let on to my tactics.

Swift and humble as a swallow, I ducked...while a thrust of wind came droning past, then hopped on its back, and rode it like a god-blamed conscience— never let it go before it hit its zenith...then hopped off to a gap in the sky, volleying to keep the level until a greater thrust came going farther out.

I rode long into the night, keeping watch for some angle to break through.

Then gradually towards the hour of dawn I mastered the bastard! My wings bit free of it. ...I had risen above!

My propellers haggard and yet feeling stronger than ever before, cleft broad circles and strutted a new felt poise. The expected fatigue vanished with the crisis.... and Fervour scintillated back....making small talk, tall promises, and strange monot'ny.

That night, now silencing, was the blackest I ever saw. The lingering sadness mingled with an arriving rhythm of calm...out on the rim were suggestions of an infant noon...and I coasted along expecting dawn to break any moment.

But dawn never came.

Into this black night rolled a luminous red cloud—a puff of brilliant red light!...And quicker than you could flip your tail around, the damned thing was followed by a colony of them!...and still others came...and soon the black night was checkered with red clouds.

The winds whirred past free of drag as a whistle. And red clouds came until they were thick as scales on a mackerel...And all the world pulsated red light!

The growing warmth was like a new word, the extended hand of a fallowed meaning. This could only mean I had progressed from the sphere of Earth to the sphere of the big wide world!

Revelling in its warm reception, my heart distilled a song,

> **How meagre
> are my wings to caress
> this world—
> which is no greater than
> my own thankfulness...**

In the immensity of concuspiscent splendour, jim's advising me to rise above took on new meanings; and I thanked him for his counsels.

Getting out to space is quite like lifting in the psyche, Red Eyes. In atmosphere one inkles with the idea; but there is still the familiar in abundance, and you haven't really left home.... A little farther out you wing into those raucous winds on the border — the perimeter of atmospheric encasement; and their intimidation poses more than the timid can endure.... But once you cross that border — get the feel of the warmth...you are airy, erect, and weightless —you discover it to be your own true destiny, and you're sure you will never turn back again ... that's space.

Everything changes.

Time changes. Light changes. Pace changes. You don't Hawk around circling on your oars any more. Space won't tolerate it.

And the rate of the pace was astounding. I lifted with incredible swiftness. For not long was I spry in this redness before its clouds burst into tones of ember ... and soon the sun seemed to go half cocked...not setting up or down, just cocked...and casting a tint like apricot twilight over and through the firmament. There was a knelling tone like a call for true reckoning...as if the Sun sat beckoning all things before its judgement... It was like some dream out of early youth to witness authentic ember — the author of autumn sunsets, cathedral bells...the glow about camp fires in the night. I thought to call it a thousand other eyes...but when I would have uttered words of it, my jaws set fixed, and I mumbled half word and witlessly through stunned lips...

Ember had entrusted her visage solely to me —

In mute astound, then, I gave reverent regard and vowed to contain the apparition and all it suggested in silence....And it lingered for awhile then caught up its skirt and tipped away...

The play of light behind me quickened in a flash!... As dreamers wake and slumber through the day clause, fomenting fragments of the deep self, I resumed the course — flying on into stacks of billowing yellowing mists, recounting the more profound assurances of Ember's fair visage.

I was free?

No, Red Eyes. I wasn't so free as I was disciplined, freedom — as I had dreamed of freedom — was a lace myth.

But I got a lot of kicks. My thighs boiled over, and for a counter I altered the shade with every change of light...

Uncap the flask, Red Eyes — my throat dries.

...I had black buttons, ember shanks, red wing bars and a matching cap...

...primrose shoulder patches, lime gazers — I was too fabulous a Hawk to squawk!

More!...Gator. I can give you the down on freedom. Freedom, supposedly Love's standing guard on Earth, is addicted to her cups and often sits drunk.

And, well ... you haven't heard the best!

I would have settled for the stars, but Fervour led me to the Sun ...

... a little bit more now ... and we will resume discourse with words of the self... ... ... from beyond the level of "selves"...

Swell!... Settle.

Swan Song Of Migration

As true lovers refrain from errant affections and are made strong, I kept within the slender lane of my own strength with fervour...

Be true!
Be beautiful...
Be free!

I bubbled, shedding every shred of sophistication. I dared believe, and cherish, let flow through my being — a nourishing and cleansing carduvial flood....I cannot well tell you all it was. No surface on Saturn, or Earth, is so vast as to contain its infinite reflection. I can more truly say what things were not....There were no doubts, no false hopes and no persuasion. There was no beginning and no end of it; it was. And — were it sustained — would make a god of you...

My mean tokens, passion, song, and artful winging— were no match for such a mantle. Still — I gave it, as one overlooking a lake serene would give his goodest thoughts...as one from the loftiest peak would make a sigh.

Wild from the rife of ecstasy, I winged each given gale as though it were my sole creation. I caroled in the ecstasy of every spiral, spontaneous praise.

"...afloat on truth
I kiss the secret of youth...
And I'd like to live—
                    forever!"

These were sound notes of a joyful voice muffled in the wrap of blessings so immense.

I lifted on and upward in great swirls of quickening light, checked only by the creeping stills of waning ecstasy.

I lifted on and upward pursuing the course as daffodil skies tensed and brightened as the belly of a lilly….and fogs of primrose sifted in, pale, and brilliant as the moon.

In such a swell of light the first other thing one perceives is the marked increase in visibility. I could see for ages and ages…and progressively the sensation of each was that of regression to greater youth and innocense and gaiety, each holding forth some truth more evident than ever before or after. I recall the vista of primrose. I thought…

"To be less than lofty is sinful; to be lifting up and out of the mire is redemption —"

Amid shafts of increasing light, I hit a plateau, a little 'high' into spirits of rum…caroling

> **Mist …**
> **You whirl of Moon!**
> **I am but one will to warmth**
> **whose wills as my own—**
>
> **That warmth is you.**

Never again was I to sing with such ease, carols were but the bit of a cup that ran over.

But the sharper the ecstasy…the sharper the pain.

As in every birth, towards the end, the most extreme, perhaps frightful in the absence of knowledge.

And the very instant you wing into such a new zone its demands are slapped on you ... such demands or laws as govern the interim status...And they are good and exacting from the level of their introduction on...

jim had a way of preparing me for demands of the up and coming zones. He would radiate an impression, or a meaning, or a symbol, to sway the imagination.

Winds, swift and respite, having brought sounds — the full range of yellow hues, ushered in tones of daunting green...and things went drab — topaz like tarnished gold....

There was, then, the sure impression of a sketchy and obscure abstraction. Its meaning:
...not what happens to your person; but what happens out of your person to...

— umph! Sounds like...the sort of dickering one would do in the composition of song, I thought, flying on...

Or perhaps a line for some other bird...one can pick up information beyond what is told to him, if the mind is sufficiently sensitive...

I parroted the line, soaring on as usual — emanating the positive, and because I really enjoyed it —

And watching the last vapors of gold fold up, as springing lime light sprawled its bastions far, silently, I marveled at the immense abilities of space...its absolute wealth, its extravagant use of light.

Then while marveling, as it were, my thoughts flashed back to the struggle for mutation and the remarks people had made...when they saw me sitting in the tree. I remembered one man, who spoke to me... just out of the blue, there was no conversation, in fact I hadn't even spoken to him...but he said to me,

What you need is to go get your-self a job...

At first I smiled: it was amusing in retrospect; I was going to laugh about it...but then I grew furious!

...the nerve of that character, and his lunch-bucket morality...to say anything!...

I could swear it was only for a second, or less; but would you believe it threw me back...

I tried to right myself quickly, and incline in some direction that would restore a sense of rise; and show jim I hadn't really meant it.

And I winged and I winged, and flap, flap, flap, — But God...! Nothing happened!

So I said to jim,

All right. You win. If I have to love those bastards, I'll love them. I'll be as excellent as I have to be. I'm not going back!

Thenceforth I commenced to rise....Fervour chuckled. And henceforth I fixed my attention to things I was sure of being positive about....

It was the day of budding ultimates. As I reviewed songs I had sung in various zones, they brought swells of light...and Fervour seemed mine forever....The windless capering—gave less caprice and more encouragement. I would not have asked greater visibility. And now I had commence distilling every thought. I was damned near about to sparkle.

Winds, swift and respite, swept out over the shady border, and back into swirls of lime.

Filled to the self's capacity...I phrased tribute to the sky's kept promises; and hoped that the brimming joy of this realization might never be less poignantly felt.

"Let me never forget...the struggles,
the pain, the fears–and the sweat...

Maintainance of the level was as simple as further self perfection, I reckoned.

I did not suspect...I could not suspect what Fervour and jim had apparently known all along.

There is a phase of steep ascent before the Sun, demanding the ultimate in purity and power, and precision. And here one learns to relent to Love, for Love is a sovereign; there are powers to be gotten only in her domain.

There lay in the outer reaches of lime, a blue abyss...filled with blue languor...laying in wait to halt and administer the ultimate in pain to all in flight, without exception.

It had the nalling power of a collapsing bridge. And I soared smack into it...

Visibility zero. Pinions languished, and paining at the faintest suggestion of continuing the flight.

jim flashed a mat —

The only defense is precision...
and Fervour slept.

My head felt as though it were the World's one podium, without sufficient wit or imagination to ponder the nature of its noises and shifting weights....Some agent had thrown a veil over the mind, dulling the sensitivity.

It was better not to think. I determined not to think; but commanded haggard propellors to spar with precision...and Spartan oblivion.

Once out of the area I would coast and let them recoup. I didn't dare fall asleep in this sleep-inducing langour. I knew the talents of rest too well. Rest out of cyclic rhythm was a whore. It would dull the sensitivity further; and you might wake up god knows where.

The abyss was a sea of enigmas. And not an eventful climb, except as a milestone in self direction.

My aching pinions trudged slothfully on under commitment...inspite of the aggravation of pain produced by every effort to pull up and out of it. All facets of mind shut down except to a fog-heavy trance...and a vague silhouette of **Her** loveliness...

Blindly, I kept plodding in the direction of up —

And long after rankling in this sea of langour, insensible to hope, gain, expectancy, and unaware of pleasure...long after giving all I could corral of effort, a glimmer of lime light penetrated the blue,...and visibility quickened...

The grip of langour commenced to give...the world stepped down!

And I cried, **Hold on, old Sky...I'm making it!**...

And I lifted...and the lifting carried to tides of greater lime...high sounding and terrifically brawn....O but the radiance! — like Spring breaking in on rugged March...

Then from an even keel in temper, sentiment and jest, I could see...there need not be so many ups and downs.

> **One can live to**
> **A level wherefrom**
> **All things become**
> **—simply delightful—**

It would seem all prior effort and perseverance were justified by a new quality of self... the bearing of an inner insistence — on consistency of poise, and therefore effect.....For this was the authentic stuff, manners — wherein they are an expression of felt beauty...and are but reflections of firm assist...

Radiation en masse changed remarkably fast. The blowing lime wed itself to cascading shades of blue...for a moment darkness. —then turned to a sparkling vert-marine - light of greater intensity and yet dim...dim like the Moon on a day it eclipses the Sun; or close enough not to vaunt itself...as do lesser reflections. But the sense of being in such proximity to the Sun is beyond the telling power of loose words.

> **Within the shadow of the sun**
> **some clapping gull sends one**
> **its fairest air to breath...**

And sweetens the existence...and
engages it well; and the state
of things is thoroughly acceptable!

And this transpiration...this April...this full eve of old hope and young delight. I pointed both wings to the Sun — whipped up! and eclipsed the very brow of ethereal rapture...

Having risen through the sea of mingling winds and wills of stratosphere, I raced on into the realm of pearly saints...pastel illamas...and April; poised for an instant above gale calls of effort, and skip — leveled to a crest of winds mingling below, content to cruise on, above, and beyond the world!

Sparkling irridescent violet splinters pierced the air with arrow-like directness, twinkling hints of every other hue....To inhale of its crisp pungent air was to indulge in essences of dreams....

My heart puffed up like a gourd blinking, joy beams and pounded acceptance ... as I piped carduvial songs:

My dearest fervour

**song is wine of the heavens
and you — wine of the earth;**

**if ever you elect to sober
the world's most intoxicated hawk**

deny me.

**...You...
the noose let down
from heaven to caress**

> *and lift me*
> *to view of all the fulness*
> *and joy — which is*
> *heaven*
>
> *Were I god,*
> *I would never dare!*
> *make you more beautiful*
> *...than you are...*

The sentiments within me welled up from ecstasy to more carduvial sensations of fulfillment.

I was a success! I knew...I could tell by the response of the Angels...

The enkindled Sun lay not so far away, couched in a nest of iridescent down...A gossamer world! with the luster of pearl...and this hue, I altered my heart.

I was for winging through — all finished! except for the bearing of jim. There were emanations of him...I knew it was he. But he hovered out a ways in the surrounding ether... implicating question or displeasure... and as though he might consider it best not to communicate.

It was remarkable and rather unsimplicated, the relationship with jim and me...a sort of self in self relationship. He took cares in my depress, and applause in my jubilation. There never was a word I needed that he didn't stand ready to read; and always we shared our thoughts without guise.

Of course, jim was not ordinarily verbal. In fact, usually in tête a tête, he radiated meanings which I later trans-phrased with words.

And so — in this nature — I held myself, in wait for the reception of some symbol or an impression.

But for this transpiration, his reluctance ebbing, jim ranged in close...and his words were as sharp as shrill cries in the dawn. He said: **Now where are you going, Hawk?...Where are you going? There is only work, there's love — there's play...Where are you going?**

It was always reassuring to have jim speak to me. And playfully, I lisped the line...**only work, there's love — there's play**...How lovely! He could say so much, so well, so simply. ...An increment — no doubt — an additional gem for my voluminous store of Cestral lore...a brighter gem to sparkle among the others...**there's only work, there's love, there is play**... Beautiful! I had a notion it meant one should engage each of these to the fullest of current capacity ... and so get the rewards of living all along, and in the nowness of things....But then — surely — I had not neglected this—

Perhaps...perhaps...having a mighty ear for great wit, this was jim's way of ribbing me for being so anxious to be...

Why, of course!!

And at the thought of me and jim now being friends enough for a bit of banter and wit ... I opened my bill and squalled and hawed...and shook my syrinx almost to pieces.....It was the best guffaw I had had for many happenings, and I whooped and cackled...and hawed and hittered...till my temples reddened and I felt like somebody else...

I had stroked very little in the violet zone. There was energy in the position and it wasn't necessary. But I whooped and cackled so hard and loud, and long, I damned near capsized.... So I swept my alulas forward and resumed the stroking...resumed the lift! I fluttered—still cackling—through the Sun's irridescent nest....And that was it!

Instantaneously I was stunned by a bolt of cross-firing energies more dazzling than the Earthen Sun!... sizzling through and about me at velocities mightier thana flash! And each was a Will, was a value, was an absolute...in fluid kosmic diamond!

Caught up in a blaze — resonant as a million hallelujahs!... I and all the world were consumed ... and the man within me died, faintly gasping, "**...my god, this is God...**"

...then swelled the purest fire of joy and wisdom
proclaiming the power of one mind over all...
declaring its being in first place and last analysis—
wanting nothing and giving all...
A joy pool of power!
eternally young!
eternally resounding flare skirts of infinity!
eternally sounding the hope of love...

In the eve of this moment, the dazzling rays
commenced to scatter.....A tottering ego staggered in the
shadows of their abandon ...and with all the wits I could
summon, I knew this to be the highest and perhaps the
last in a series of lessons for me.

Simultaneously I thought to describe the diamond
wills in song and imprint them on the integument of
my breast and, with sensuous claws, struggled to arrest
at least a decalogue. to this day, under the moult of my
bosom, they are still carven veins...

You want me to sing them? All right, I'll sing them
for you; but first get something I can use for a muffler.

Go on, get something! What d'you think I want to
do — **"Whistle all creatures rumbling into the river"?**

Never fan a flame
that tempers implements to ends
beyond
fully engaged and fully reissued
opportunities

Every beingness
projects
from super Kosmic
consciousness—

And none
are ignored or forgotten
either in total
or particular evolutions

Lend to every occurrence
 the assertion of its chance
    to matter

Force nothing!
... let things transpire ...

Intuition must be met
    with recognition and respect...
Work swiftly with it!
Work silently with it!

Love ...
the much sought

mundane delight
is conceived in need;
And approaches perfection
to the extent each lover
finds his imperfection
complemented by the other

Despite involvings
—binding—
one life process
to another;
Each remains
a singular process
and will evolve as such.

The reflective giver
is the true receiver.

Take no more than
is given

Transcendence
the rising above
zones priorly known
in descent
hinges to
—the quality—
of one's performance

It was a moment of excellence I would have held some little sparks from. My talons involuntarily took to the task...and were scrawling impetuously long after the last diamond arrow smote its way through the sky's veiled dome...untouched, untold, and unforgettable...

If only for such an instant as to make it seem nocturnal, it remains forever beyond measure. For I witnessed the shape of things ... through the eyes of immutable oneness; and was free — to the maximum — of work and love and play, for as long as I lived...and remembered.

Earth Electric

I thought most now of Mankind, as I remembered him — and of Earth...'mm Earth electric. Of man plodding on through the cold of small existence...and by the **light** of small existence. And suddenly it was clear to me. Man's problem is **he cannot see...he cannot see!**

Every Man has instruments for making a proper thing of his existence. But — ironically — it is only as he approaches perfection are they of any avail...

I did not resist the growing compassion for Man. More-over, as I thought of him my breast welled full with kindred identity...and ached...and it came to me... that... I ought to go back.

What is actual in Man's sphere, and what appears to be — in the light of imperfection —are not at all equal. They are, in fact, so grossly **unequal** one scarcely resembles the other ... considering all odds, it seemed remarkable he does so well...and I knew I **must** regress to Earth electric.

Man was sent to Earth because the day was in ignorance and wanted bringing into violet cognizance...

Man — to Earth its only seed for highest aspiration — germinates small stalks that lift... when full grown... into the heart of knowledge, and blosson there! that **Love** may flow through their petals to **all** the Earth...and quicken its pulse...elevate Man's existence — and enjoy full sway ...!

... O could I get back...Unto Me — I would call each floundering Soul...

... those **ilsated** *with success — despairing — like scum seeing itself only as scum, unrelated to Earth's essential terrestrial successes...the wild eyed* **domesticated**, *paying in delirium and thankless sweat the never-ending ransom of stymied growth. Only! domestication knows the heavy steps of the down-plodden...the* **roused** *and the* **awakened** *— ignoring counsel of the mind's eye...their commitments thereof blown along the littoral, and thus the greater strides... the* **innocent** *in a sea which detains not the innocent... and souls washed* **on the rocks** *with dead shells out of the sea...*

...every mark...of the wayward seems like eternal sand — **If I could get back I would embrace each one, and to make them** *— as vivid as the Sun — the significance of Man's existence...of his being in stream with source.*

In the dankest humour of a living soul, there is hope that Man — yet in stream with source — may flower...

Mucus is hope; and matter scattered energy...

Death is suspected the dourest evil on Earth, and avoided like the threat of a witch...I would give him the more availing fear of wasting fluidity on inane dissensions, and making — of their differences — insufferable monsters.

Hope willed that men would not augment each other in evolving towards violet cognizance. The deed of this will dwells in their dissimilarities.

And War, I could see, was not inherent to the lot of Man. War — as **Peace** — has claim to a level in the range of human action. And even assumes beauty when seen as one of the gifts of many choices: red – ember – primrose – or violet — There can be no sense in quarreling with a valid stratum! The only way out of it is out! This is no less true of my own flock. Many a tide as I am homing to Saturn I find them slumbering in a calm which is not **peace**, which settles only to knowledge … and I grouse so loud as to startle them! Or I ruffle my plummage with the fury of rain! They cannot…they must not-settle to **presumed peace**. There is too much yet to learn! They are born! to inherit full existence. … I thought I would unveil before Man the one anima of all form — Cosmic Radiation — and truly on Earth, it is as a saint of pearl…The blind, charmed by the ramp of her footsteps, speak in glowing terms of **Radiation**. The deaf, bewitched by the flambouyance of her smile toast **Colour**…and everywhere, **Instruments — salute… in quest of Truth's behest** whispering **Light** — Yet she, as the Sun, is one perfect beauty emitting myriad leads to Truth. Where she lingers knowing hosts fête her with fingers ungrasping. Where she runs, she would lead one to Truth more swiftly…I recalled Man's romantic watch of Sun risings, and Sun settings, Moons on the wax and Moons on the wane….the harvests of Autum and the growths of spring.

It was his understanding of light, darkness, change, fertility and sterility…but he further infused the stirrings with the authorship of Time; and assumed it all necessarily went on forever! Time is colour, flare skirts of an infinity. Time implies space between one and his cosmic source. Time measures space within the influence of a Sun. And Time is annihilated...wherever God puts out a light!

Gape at me, Gator...but can't you see, I had to go back!

I tipped my wings and attempted to parachute down...but there was a gilted mist suspended all around....No flip of the tips availed a swift change. I had to wind my way through it slowly...

A windless splendour, sprawling far like the murky radiations of a dying Sun. And so very illuminating it rendered my own form virtually invisible. If there were other beings they too were no imposition on the eyes, it was a garden pale and wind less...

I regarded the impaling mist a device to keep sojourners for a thorough consideration of the choices.

It was a garden pale...surrounding the sweet pit of the summit of **Peace**. And every herb, and path, and flower shaped of the same sweet substance. Impaled to perfect wisdom, and comfort, and bliss, there was no need to roam, for this was the state towards which all others aspire, others could only offer inferior comfort.

Having all, it wanted nothing ... and possessing no shadowy lanes, memory was obsolete. In its eyes all things moved in right order. The merest complaint becomes an attempt to confuse this order

It was a garden pale...granted the rights of ultimate sufficiency. Love's scepter was its scepter...her wisdom its wisdom, and her cup, its cup...

And I might have stayed for infinniums yet to

come. Getting back to Earth meant nothing less than beginning another tour, to be brought to a similar end.... But my thoughts remained reminiscent of Earth.

...dedicated to the unsimplicated lot of Sapiens, I would return.

I propped my wings like oars and backed out of the area as fast as I could. I had to get back!...I would show mankind the way. When he tired along the journey I would comfort him from my score of Kosmic lore, with telling pictures of the goal...

And surely, never again...would I be as susceptible as he.

OPERATION: INSPIRATION MINUS

Luxuriating in such security as can only inspire neglect, I proceeded to get downright careless. I violated one of the principles garnered on my breast...Then **Fervour**, the strength of my wings took flight. And I drifted in the direction of waning light.

Minds within me commenced to sleep...and all save grumbling was nalled to glum.

But regression is a hurtful proposition...More wine...

No matter how willfully elected, its hurtful. The more you are aware of it, the more it hurts. It was like severing my own propellers.

In command of the maneuver stood adamant Free Will; the mind proved most flexible over many involved assignments. Of necessity, it tyrannized the Will to Survive, which has but one idea — progression; and the latter proved no docile gulping.

> **Are you mad?**
and fresh painful was its cadence,
> **Can I ... Should I?**
> **having known life**
> **in fullest fire**
> **settle for an inferior**
> **proposition?**
> **You go honking with me**
> **into a realm reserved**
> **for gods;**
> **And when you showed your rump,**

I — alone — pay the penalty
for your intrusion ...
Your never again
finding ecstasy again
in lots apportioned
to your kind.

...Keep the cup full...

Free Will pondered the protest, briefly;
but then brought it along anyway, without debate as he
would an unknowing and petulant squabbling.

But the fervour under whose spell I winged to violet
heights was gone; the rum of ecstasy that sustained
me inflight...gone. Only comparable ache replaced the
ecstasy I had known was mine forever. It seemed
senseless — in brief spells — to carry on with this.
Assuredly, I would be super to sapiens...a helm to the
prow of their endeavours. But what for me? A super
solitaire with diamond memories?

I tell you there is no ache like the ache in wake of
regression.

Promise of Earth

When I could detect the vibrations of jim, I gave him a line of sheer insolence; and mocked the eerie, desolate spaces attending the descent.

Where is the 'Me'
and my living?
Is it this roaming
—ghost free—
knowingness?
Without night or day
... centurial stay,
Allegiance to City or Continent?

Am 'I' just the peg
that brings it close to Earth?
Is this my existence
...pegging awarenesses to Earth?
Is this the sum of things
that is the 'Me'?

Only the promise of Earth held hope in such terrifying moments of nothingness. At least it offered form, problems, brakes.

Many an elegant sensation too silent and too sincere for words waited this descent. And I nursed the spiraling, hearing occasionally a faint **if only I could rise above**....But once across the red border, it was operation accelerando.

My heart danced with anticipation and recall as I glimpsed the first littoral of a northern shore....Once more I would settle to Earth...dear old Earth ...

My wings were greater than the task. I stalled over the coast — throwing all propellers into reverse. ... And in less than a finished second, I settled — braking with *rapacious skill ... feeling myself power ... and bearing the supernal counsel of the Kosmos:* **Omniscience is not the proper burden of mankind!... but magnificence is...**

A glare of crimson flung itself around the horizon.... Fierce breakers had beat the rock into ridges and troughs; and — squalling still — dashed sprays up over the coast!

I broadened my nares to inhale more deeply the air and looked — with fascination — out over the sea. Full gales fetched spectacular waves, some whose crests leaped the **height of hills and** *poised before scattering their masses — the dash wash* **of waters back to sea.** *The hue of crimson through the gusting sprays, over scrubbed rocks, and the pounding surflent Earth an enchantment I shall never forget...And I drank of the bluishwaters.*

Nary a yesterday — nor a tomorrow — could vamp me into wedding any singular situation. Infinity, having been a mere experience, was the natural range for me. I was too mighty to be less than free. Virtue — a piecemeal tangent off the **casual.** *I brought along a subservient guard. And for all rumblings on Earth about* **justice,** *to me it was an incumbent gratuity.*

The future lay its naked form prostrate before me, knowing I could gratify every need. ... I ruffled my feathers! and the flying mist...assembled the image of a rainbow!

Goodwill *— I wound on a string wherefore to use. And everywhere I stanced and pranced ... stalked and walked — something of a gilted mist fell about me,*

in fact, *there was just* **Me**...*and God—and* **I** *was magnificent.... ....*

But magnificence is a condition...like the blues, neglect, abuse, pain, or shock. It's just the aura off the process beneath it...and Freedom is like running grass.

This has stripped me to the soul, and you've told it to me — What happened?

Wait, Gator...you'll know. Hold up off the flask...

Freedom is a process — in pursuit of a type of excellence on its own...well on its own.

It can't make carefree of a single moment. It's gotta keep moving! and making choices —

**Freedom carries a spear, pointed
for precision
of brash selection**

And it's no damned inner impulse either. I mean it is not ordinarily met with recognition or respect...still it's gotta keep moving and making choices.

No matter how it's banged around, disbelieved, or disrespected, Freedom must maintain its brand of excellence.....Freedom gives long before it gets.

But it operates with imprezistence — that is within the framework of immutable codes of change...suffering neither more nor less control. The most self impairing thing it can do is control a situation.

Why?...
Watch, Gator, what I say now: Truth is the angel

of Freedom. Within and via the structure of Kosmic principles — she makes every appropriation, advantage, and pleasure. But she is adamant if ignored. The very same instant you set up your own controls Truth stops—WHAP! That's a new word they've got for really...

Truth and the appropriated...a distended circle — neater than Steven — Watch this:

There is no insistence in Truth on equality, I would dare suggest Truth abhors equalities. The artistry of Truth could not persist in equalities ... her cue is cause. There is a valid cause — why all things exist in Truth; and as each authentic cause evokes its own appropriations — and they do! one may discover Truth by precise avail and use of appropriations given...

What happened! Come on, now...What happened!

...it was a dismal choice, Red Eyes...Few believed I flew out to space in the first place.

Then — when one returns to Earth, he does involve... and he is susceptible...and powerful, compassionate, and hopeful, but people inadvertently serve the forces which detain and he meets with much disregard, neglect and abuse, and disbelief, and it's painful.

If he's not very careful he gets more hard knocks than anybody...because the least he can accept is the most Earth offers...goodness, beauty — truth — and dignity —

Lavender! Great!

...lavender, yes...But no one told me, the only crutch for such a process is extrospection — certain disillusion — certain equilibrium between the inner and outer awarenesses...Such balance is only kept as Freedom keeps the lead; but Freedom has none but the one damned crutch!

Freedom — our spear
must know itself our spear!
For if Freedom sleeps,
Love is raped

The play in Freedom is to be free from fangs of fear, hate, anxiety — and greed. The trick is to stay free from...Then one can swoop — rapaciously — to one encounter...ascending with ease to safer heights! ever maintaining himself for another...the most exciting, daring, and dangerous existence in the world!

Say what? **How did I expect to get away with that on Earth?**

The provisions for such living are there. They are like beams of reason under constant protection of Kosmic guards...and really — on them — there is no limit where you can go or what you can do. But if you get **off**... Gator, you're just off, unless you can get back on again. And there is no ritual that makes it less real. There is no excuse that detains Truth.

No, Gator. Don't say these things are debatable — no! Truth is! Truth **is**! whether you're up to it or down to it or not.... Truth IS!

But your dis-illusion can go up in blue smoke any time. All you have to do is forget that. And Freedom has none but the one damed smudge...forgetfulness.

> **One must be the center, its strength**
> **and defender;**
> **What there is of God with Man**
> **is within Man**

You **can't see that**?...ha'....The other day, in happy smiles, I met Jack Inkling. Now... you can't see me think all the time; but Jack Inkling can....

Freedom — then subsuming Truth and...Truth and... ...Truth and extr'spec! tion...ha, hear that? you hear that? ... Hell, it's no mode for a serious carefree.

> **The biggest word out of civility**
> **so far as words symbolize concepts—**
> **is responsibility**

Responsibility. ... Did I ever tell you about res'sponsibility?... ... ... bearing the enlightened message of the Kosmos... ... ...

God-man! don't shove so... ...I am not tight, I'm just tiring a little. God! Can't you tell the difference between fight and tired? God!... ...You will hear the end of this story. Don't worry. I am the very sense of involvements.... ... ...very sense of involvements. ...Then I cannot! I will not! ... abuse the sentiment of Rest. It is the weight of work to be done that creates the sensation of want for rest, you know.....But work must be done and this story told before I presume to rest.

Magnificence then, subsuming Truth and ex... stropec...shun... ... even the Moon's orbit would make less sense if we went through all the unsimplicated minutia of its journey...

I shan't sleep in the woods tonight! ♫
I found a log in the mauve moonlight.

All right...All right!... ...
"Can't sleep" shan't have anything to do with it... and
don't shove... ... ...

Listen, Red Eyes...when you grow weary of your
culture commas and break through their restrictions...
BOOM!...you will break into a bright new exhilarating
realm of greater responsibility, by greater ex-
tr'-spection, by greater participation, by greater
compensation. ... That is if you make it...GR x GE x GP
x GC = Freedom = Magnificence!

Pardon me for being so demonstrative...but this
equation is loaded...HIC!...

I could tell this one story in terms of the creation...
or give you the literal facts with built in legatos....I
could make it a high-sounding sermon on Divine art in
mortal desperation ... You do believe that I am wise?...
and worldly?

But to render it pure and mythic ... this iridescent
heart, this lift to the Sun, this April in ecstasy ... and
magnificence in gold ... I was the one night and the
several day... ... ...
... ...in love... ... ...

But we will close with statements from... ...an old...
pal of mine...I cannot leave.... I cannot leave.... I
cannot... ... ... leave...

The log...Red Eyes, the log...

www.ingramcontent.com/pod-product-compliance
Lightning Source LLC
LaVergne TN
LVHW070853011125
824778LV00063B/1848